Who Hides Here?
Footprints
On The Farm

Written by Rachel Coverdale
Illustrated by Shelly Oyston
United Kingdom edition

For Lincoln, our very own farm animal - RC

For Oliver - SO

First published 2019 by Willow Breeze Publishing
Text Copyright © Rachel Coverdale 2018
Illustrations copyright © Shelly Oyston 2019
Moral rights asserted.
FIRST EDITION 2019
The right of Rachel Coverdale to be identified as the author of this work has been asserted by her in accordance with the Copyright, Designs and Patents Act 1988. All rights reserved.
ISBN: 978-1-9161080-0-4
A CIP catalogue record for this book is available from the British Library
No part of this publication may be reproduced or transmitted in any form or by any means electronic, or mechanical, including photocopying, recording, or by any information storage and retrieval system, without permission in writing from the author.
NOTE TO READERS:
Farms are private land and to trespass is against the law. Animals can be dangerous; children must be supervised at all times.

Dear Grown-Up,

Please insert a picture or drawing of your child

on the last page of this book. Alternatively,

you can place a piece of shiny silver paper

to act as a mirror.

Dear Child,

We hope you enjoy discovering the animals from the clues. Hopefully, you will find real animal footprints when exploring the countryside.

Who is hiding on the farm?

Sometimes shelters in a barn.

A coat like silk,

We drink her milk.

Who is hiding on the farm?

"It is me," moos cow noisily.

Who is hiding in the pen?

She loves to make a muddy den.

A curly tail,

A fallen pail.

Who is hiding in the pen?

"It is me," grunts pig hungrily.

Who is hiding in the hay?

Likes to nibble, scurry and play.

His long tail

Leaves a trail.

Who is hiding in the hay?

"It is me," chitters rat merrily.

Who is hiding behind the door?

Stamping hooves upon the floor.

You decide

To stroke or ride.

Who is hiding behind the door?

"It is me," neighs horse triumphantly.

Who is hiding among the reeds?

Eating worms and seeds and weeds.

Fly, swim or walk,

But cannot talk.

Who is hiding among the reeds?

Who is hiding on the hill?

Often standing very still.

Eats grass till full,

And gives us wool.

Who is hiding on the hill?

"It is me," bleats sheep gleefully.

Who is hiding near the pond?

When you know him, you'll grow fond.

A slimy skin,

Inflatable chin.

Who is hiding near the pond?

Who is looking in the mirror?

Come up close, nearer and nearer.

Who can you see?

It's you or me.

Who is looking in the mirror?

"It is me," you chuckle cheerily.

This is Sammy Snail. He has photo-bombed every picture. Have another look through the book – can you find him?

Do you know the Country Code?

- ✓ Always stay on footpaths
- ✓ Never leave litter
- ✓ Close gates after you
- ✓ Do not approach the animals
- ✓ Keep dogs on leads

Charlotte sheep knows her wool will be made into pretty colours, but she would like you to colour her in now. She can be any colour you wish.

Can you join the footprints to the animals?

The best way to see farm animals is to visit a petting farm.

If you get the chance to go, why not take this book and circle any animals you see?

www.ingramcontent.com/pod-product-compliance
Lightning Source LLC
Chambersburg PA
CBHW042030100526
44587CB00029B/4354